ACE RIZOTI

SALES SECRETS

**The Ultimate Guide to the Art of Selling,
Learn Savvy Salesmanship and Sales Techniques
That Would Let You Sell Ice to Eskimos**

Descrierea CIP a Bibliotecii Naționale a României
ACE RIZOTI
   SALES SECRETS. The Ultimate Guide to the Art of Selling, Learn Savvy Salesmanship and Sales Techniques That Would Let You Sell Ice to Eskimos / Ace Rizoti – Bucharest: Editura My Ebook, 2021
   ISBN

ACE RIZOTI

SALES SECRETS

**The Ultimate Guide to the Art of Selling,
Learn Savvy Salesmanship and Sales Techniques
That Would Let You Sell Ice to Eskimos**

My Ebook Publishing House
Bucharest, 2021

ACE RIZOTI

SALES SECRETS

The Ultimate Guide to the Art of Selling,
Learn the Skills and Tips of Salespeople Who Know
that I Should Listen to Sell and Sell to Make

TABLE OF CONTENTS

FOREWORD

Is it very possible to sell ice to an Eskimo? This is one question that many people have always asked themselves. The answer is yes. It possible to sell ice to the Eskimos depending on the sales skills you have.

If you are a good salesman, you can do this without much hassle. A person who is well skilled in the art of selling can sell anything to anyone and make good cash out of it at the end. Knowing how to sell is the basic to selling anything. It will determine if the business will be successful or a failure.

There are some secrets which you need to read so that you get to know what it takes to have that convincing power that will see you sell ice to the Eskimos. If you don't have these secrets, then you are missing out on a great opportunity of making good cash. These are the basics of earning big and you can learn them in this eBook.

After reading this eBook you will learn on how you can sell ice to Eskimos without much hassle. You will be equipped with all the skills needed to be a good sales man who will convince people buy anything. This will see you make huge profits.

Sales skills are not inborn. They are built over time. This is why you need to take your time to go through the eBook so that you get to know the right skills that you need to have to convince Eskimos buy what they don't like-ice.

You don't need to go to sales and marketing courses to convince the Eskimos buy ice. With this eBook, you will get to know the secrets that have been hidden for ages that will help you sell ice to Eskimos.

There are a number of tips that have been used by many successful sales people which you need to be aware of so that you successfully convince the Eskimos to buy ice from you.

If you become aware of these steps, you will be on the road to riches as you will make good cash by convincing the Eskimos to buy ice.

This eBook has been written in very simple English that you will find easy to read and understand. You will for really find it quite interesting if you are interested in getting good salesmanship skills.

Savvy Salesmanship

Master The Art Of Selling Ice To Eskimos With The Greatest Sales Techniques In The Universe

Chapter 1

Who Are the Eskimos?

In this chapter, you will be exposed to information on who the Eskimos are and their way of life. You will also learn how they come to be and where they live.

❖ Learning about the Eskimo will be of great help to you as a sales person. This is because you will get to know the kind of people you will be dealing with.

❖ Learning on the geographical location of Eskimos and their way of life will equip you with skills on how you are going to convince them buy ice. These are people who live on a very cold climate. Will you manage to sell them ice? Find the answers to this question in this eBook.

Who Are The Eskimos?

Eskimo is an American word meaning 'eater of raw meat'. Eskimos are people whose origin is thought to be from northern parts of Asia. They migrated from this place to the north of America in the modern day Alaska. They then dispatched into various parts of this continent. In the modern day they live in four areas:

➤ The Soviet Union

➤ Greenland

➤ The United States (Alaska) and

➤ Canada.

Eskimos are people who share similar physical characteristics. They are light skinned people who have black hair, dark eyes and a wide face with the cheekbones being high. They use the same language. These are people who live in the cold areas near the Arctic Circle. These are people who have weathered the cold storms to survive. This is a very challenging climate that only the fittest will survive.

What is the lifestyle of Eskimos?

In order to full understand how the Eskimos survive, it is good to learn their way of life in terms of food, shelter, clothing etc.

In terms of food, the cold waters water of the area they live provides them with good food to keep them going. They mostly rely on the seal. This is their staple food for a long time. They also hunt salmons, cods, whales and other sea animals for food. During the summer, the Eskimos hunt for caribou and geese. During the winter they could opt for polar bears, foxes, and hares. These are people who mostly rely on seal, caribou and the skin of the whales.

The seal which provides a stable food source for the Eskimos.

When it comes to shelter, the Eskimos have a changing pattern of shelter because they are ever on the move. This is because they keep moving from one place to another looking for food. During the summer, they could use skins from seals and caribous to build tents where they could sleep. When winter came, they would build snow houses. These houses were built by snow blocks. These houses are built in a spiral shape. These are houses mainly referred to as igloo.

'Igloo' a house for the Eskimos during their stay in the cold areas. It is made from blocks of ice. Picture gotten from Luxurylaunches.com

The clothes used by the Eskimos are made from animal skins. The caribou skin is the favorites of many. This is because this skin is lightweight but very warm. They also used skins of the seal, polar bear and the Arctic fox. These clothes were styled in different ways depending on the region. In most cases, the clothes are designed in the form of a hooded jacket, trousers, socks and boots. During the winter the kind of clothes that are used are made of two layers. The inner layer made from fur and the outer layer that has been made of skin. Between the two layers was air that could be used to keep the body warm.

The Eskimos wore thick clothes made from animal skins. Picture gotten from whatjamiefound.com

The Eskimos lived in families that were in terms of hundreds of people. These families consisted of a husband, wife and children. The man's role was to look for food, drive dog sled and built shelters.

Wives were given the role of making clothes and cooking for the family.

Rules That Governed The Stay Of Eskimos

The Eskimos had no laws but they had rules of conduct that guided them in their daily living. The two most important rules were:

1. All members should help each other
2. Each person should have a peaceful stay in relation to others. 3.

Those who refused to abide by this rules were neglected in the society. They were despised but then treated humanely as they were given food by other family members.

The Eskimos believed in spirits that were controlled by the wind, sun and the moon. Their prime god was Sedna who they believed had power over the seals, whales, and all other sea animals. They also believed that animals and human beings had souls that lived after dead. They buried their death by covering them with stones after wrapping them in an animal skin.

In the modern world, the Eskimos live a different life. Most of them are now living in towns. They have also changed their mode of dressing in that they can now wear modern clothes and eat food bought from stores. They have also stopped using dog sleds and instead they use motorboats and snowmobiles. Most of them have received modern education and have got formal employment.

Chapter 2

Selling Ice to the Eskimos

In chapter one, we learnt who the Eskimos are. By now you got enough clues on the kind of people you are going to deal. You have known their life. In this chapter you will learn:

➤ The factors to consider before you start the business of selling ice to Eskimos

➤ How to sell the ice to the Eskimos

➤ The tips to selling ice to the Eskimos

Sales

Factors To Consider Before You Venture Into The Business Of Selling Ice To The Eskimos

If you are interested to venture into the business of selling ice to the Eskimos, then you need to be well prepared. This is one of the challenging businesses but which is very profitable if you sail through. In addition to your skills you need to consider other things so that you are successful.

The Market:

The market consists of the people you will be selling the ice to. In this case your market is the Eskimos. These are the target customers you are going to deal with. It is good to know the form of ice they want. This will be a good way of delivering them the right form that will see you get enough profits.

Demand:

Demand is what is needed. Before you carry your ice to the Eskimos, it is good to know if they will really need it. Know their demand i.e. the quantity they want. You should know how many people are living in a given area so that you make estimates of the quantity they may need. There are factors that may affect the demand for the ice by the Eskimos:

- ✓ Your marketing tactics
- ✓ The quality of the ice you are selling
- ✓ The price of the ice
- ✓ The amount of money the consumers have

It is good to know how these factors may affect the price of the ice.

Location:

It is good to know where you will be selling your ice. Also know the location of your business. It is good to know a good place where the Eskimos live so that you locate your ice selling business there. The Eskimos are people who like moving from place to place. This is why you need to take your time so that you know a central place where they stay for long.

Transportation:

You should consider the cost of transporting the ice to the Eskimos. The fact that ice is heavy calls for need to know the means and the cost of transporting it to the customers. It is good to know if the means of transport will be the most appropriate so that your ice is delivered safely to the customers.

How To Sell Ice To An Eskimo

The question of how would one sells ice to an Eskimo is a very challenging one. This is because under normal circumstances, we have known the Eskimos as people who live in a very cold area and ice is known to be very cold in nature. This is where the challenge arises. You can't sell people what they don't like. You will need to have some skills to convince the Eskimos to buy your products.

The first thing you will need is to be a good salesman. A good salesman is the one who has good convincing skills that will see you sell ice to the Eskimos. It will be of great significance to avoid using the term Eskimos as it shows racism and most of the Eskimos hate it. It is good to be warm and smile so that you create a good rapport with your customers. It is good to be what they are and appreciate what they have. This is the only thing that will see you succeed in selling ice to them.

It is good to get into the homes of these people. There is no successful business that has ever been held on the road. It is good to let them know your purpose with a smile. As you enter their house, be smiling and tell them why you have come. Let them know that you have come to solve their ice needs. By mentioning this, they will welcome you in and let you explain your business ideas. It is good to score before the game begins. This will be a good way of winning them to buy ice as you pocket profits.

To ensure you get good sales, it is good to hammer your strong points and the merits of your product. Ensure you pamper them with the benefits they will get from using your products. It is good to have sample products to show them. The Eskimos always dig deep into the ground to get the crystal clear ice. You can come with crystal clear ice and explain to them how it will save them on the energy and time. Try to convince them that if you sell them this ice, they will have time to do other important things like looking for food.

It is good to capitalize on facts and use them full to your advantage. It is good to introduce yourself with catchy phrases and quotes that will get their attention to you. Tell them on how your ice is different from theirs. For example, show them how it will keep them warm if they use it to build their houses. Show them how your iced tea is different from theirs. These are facts that you can use o convince them buy your product.

It is good to be jovial when marketing your ice. Try to put smiles here and there. It is also good to know the first name of the customer and capitalize on it. Try to impress them so that they get to know your products.

What You Need To Successfully Sell Ice To The Eskimos *PERSISTENCE*:

It is good not to listen to the word NO. Impossibility should not exist in your vocabulary. Don't give up on persuading the Eskimos to buy your ice. Let "no" be an opportunity to convince the Eskimos to say "yes." It is good not to listen to the prophets of 'no' and instead try and keep knocking and at last the door will be opened for you. A good sales man should never give but instead should work on the ways of convincing the customers to say yes.

Persistent is the most important key to success in any business that you venture into. The little things and ideas you pursue each day will one day reach a tipping point that will see you gain from them. This is why you need to be persistent. Picture courtesy of TJ's weblog.

CONVICTION:

It is good to act like you have achieved your aim. Convince your mind that you have managed to convince the Eskimos buy your ice. This will give you the confidence of getting to convince them in real. It is good to have that positive feeling that you have managed to convince the Eskimos to buy your ice. You can achieve this if you are ready to build some business confidence in you. Sell your ideas with a passion.

RESPECT:

This is the key to success in any business venture you have. If you treat people with respect they will also treat you with the same. It is good to remember that the first perception matters a lot. This is why you need to show the Eskimos respect from the first day you approach them. It is of great significance to appreciate their way of life. Don't underrate them due to their lifestyle. If you want to succeed in selling them ice you should not intimidate them.

Creativity is also needed for you to successfully sell ice to the Eskimos. It is good to be calculative in the way you handle things. Think of the problems the Eskimos may be facing and come up with novel solutions that will help them. Try to come up with improvised ice that will offer solutions to certain problems these people may be facing. This will be a good way of selling your ice. It is good to explain to them how you have always thought of this problem and how you arrived at this solution. This is something you need to explain with creativity so that you win them.

Another way of selling ice successfully to the Eskimos is by going crazy. By going crazy doesn't mean you get out of your mind. It means you try what has not been tried. Many people think that ice can't be sold to the Eskimos because it can't be sold. This is small thinking. The reason why ice has not been sold to the Eskimos is because it has not been tried. Be bold enough and take the bull by the horns and try selling ice to the Eskimos. This may seem an impossible mission but with determination you will make it. If you fail first time, try again. Don't give up. Try and try, again and again. You will at last make it. Take one step at a time and you will make it.

Taking one step at a time will see you achieve what you want. This is the key to success of any business. You need to start from a low place and then rise up the ladder.

Chapter 3

How to Sell Ice to the Eskimos

In chapter two you have learnt on what you need to sell ice to the Eskimos. In this chapter you will get to know how the whole process of selling ice can be done successfully.

❖ The Art Of Selling Ice To The Eskimos

❖ Laws You Need To Obey To Sell Ice Effectively To The Eskimos

The Process

The sales process of any product can be quite challenging. It involves a combination of art, science, personality and luck. This is the same case with the sale process of ice. It involves you being aggressive to convince people buy your ice. To make the whole process of selling ice to Eskimos a success, you will be required to have strategy of carrying out this business. This is a very dynamic business that has a number of challenges you will need to be keen to overcome them.

Knowing the benefits you will get from selling ice to the Eskimos is one thing that will see you work hard towards seeing the business flourish. This will be a good thing that will motivate you to use any means available to convince the Eskimos buy your ice.

Many people will be surprised if you tell them that you want to sell ice to the Eskimos. They will think you are insane by selling products that people don't need. Some may conclude that you don't have good personality to convince people buy other products so that is why you have opted for ice. You need to motivate yourself and prove them wrong by selling ice to Eskimos the same business they thought you were mad venturing into. Let no one be a roadblock to your ideas of selling ice.

To succeed in selling ice to the Eskimos, you will need to know of what benefit will be the ice to your target customers. For the sale process to be successful you will need to:

A. Understand the problems of your customers

B. Show your customers how your product in this case ice will help in addressing their problems

C. Help the customers understand how you are going to use your product to solve their problem and be available for consultation.

The kind of ice you have will market itself. It is good to have a good relationship with the customers. This relationship is built by you having high quality ice that will be of help to the customer. It is advisable you have empathy, ethic and desire.

These are the three skills you need to have so that you effectively solve the problems of the clients. If you will be able to capitalize on the three factors, you will be able to comfortably sell ice to the Eskimos. These are the three factors that a good sales man should have in mind.

The bottom line of any product is that it cannot sell itself without the salesman advertising its benefits. This is why you need to take an initiative of marketing your ice. This is because products don't deliver the selling point above on their own; they need people to market them. You will need to have good marketing skills that will see you market this ice to the Eskimos.

It is good to have the best techniques so that you effectively sell this ice to the Eskimos. If you have the best techniques you will be able to sell the ice to a number of clients. This is a good way that will see you earn good cash in a short period of time. It is good to capitalize on any selling opportunity so that you make great money.

It is good to persist even if your ideas are rejected. Take your time to persist customers so that they see you are serious to sell ice to them. Take advantage of any slightest opportunity to persuade the Eskimos to buy ice from you. Don't give up even if you are in a state of making losses.

It is good to first do good research to know if the Eskimos will buy the ice you are selling. Know if they are qualified to buy ice. It will be a waste of resources and time to go to sell ice to people who are not interested to buy. It is therefore advisable you take your time and visit the Eskimos location and know their need for ice. Prior visitation before the real sale starts will be good to help you know the Eskimos need when it comes to ice. It is good to learn about your customers and their needs.

A good ice salesman knows when to move on. It is not good to keep gloating over success. It is also good to avoid wasting time with people you think will not buy your ice. Try to convince them and if they prove impossible, move on to the next group of Eskimos who are interested with your ideas. It is good to know when to move on.

It is good to explain how different your ice is. It is advisable to explain to the Eskimos how different your ice is from the one sold by your competitors. To do this, you need to have good bargain skills. Tell them what makes you better than your competitors.

Tell them on the means you are going to use to deliver the best. It is also good to tell them what will make you be consistent in giving them the best products. When you are able to explain what makes you unique, you will be in a state to sell your ice successfully to the Eskimos.

Forming good relations with the Eskimos is another thing that will see you sell them ice successfully. After you have formed good relations, it is good to turn them to partnerships. It is good to give your customers good value which will encourage them to buy ice from you. This is one thing that will see you have potential customers to buy your ice.

The Art Of Selling Ice To The Eskimos

Before you venture into the business of selling ice to the Eskimo it is good to do your homework so that you know what you need to sell ice effectively. Just like any other business, it is good to take your time to look for the market of your products. Good preparation is one of the ways of making your business grow. It is good to have confidence in what you want to venture into. Even if you don't have experience, you can still become a savvy salesman.

Before you venture into this business with the Eskimos, it is good to know what you want from the deal. It is not good to rush. Take your time to know the main reason you want to start ice selling to the Eskimos. Most people will venture into this business to make money.

It is good to get help and information before you start selling ice to the Eskimos. This is the way that will see you succeed in your business. Seek assistance from professionals like accountants and lawyers. Other people you can't miss to consult are bankers. These are the people who will see you succeed in the business of selling ice. You can get the services of these people by making use of the internet technology.

It is of great importance to plan for the downside. It is good to know how to curb the challenges you may face. Gauge yourself to know if you are in a state to resist any drawbacks to see you succeed. It is good to use tools like insurance and bonds so that in case of losses you are compensated.

Laws You Need To Obey To Sell Ice Effectively To The Eskimos

The first law you need to know is that you should build good credibility with the customers before you sell. Make your customers trust you and the kind of ice you will sell them. This can be achieved if you sell your ideas well. If the Eskimos trust your ice, they will buy it more and more as you earn good cash.

Asking questions and listening to your customers is another law you need to abide by to sell your ice effectively. It is good to understand what the Eskimos need in order to improve their lifestyle. This will be easier to make you sell them the right ice to satisfy their needs.

It is good to position yourself as a problem-solver in the heart of the Eskimos. The way the Eskimos will think of you and your ice when you are not present matters a lot. It determines how they will respond to you when you come. When the Eskimos view you as a problem solver in terms of ice, they will readily buy it from you.

Always aim to be the best sales man in the ice selling industry. This is what will drive you to use any means to convince the Eskimos to buy your ice. It is good to attend sales seminars so that you get the right skills and experience to sell your ice to the Eskimos. Never stop improving your sales skills.

It is good to have goals and work on them if you want to succeed in selling ice. It is good to write down on the number of Eskimos you want to sell ice to per day or per week. This is one thing that will motivate you to sell ice effectively.

Chapter 4

Convincing Eskimos to Buy Ice

In chapter two, you have learnt on how to make the sale process successful. In this chapter, you will learn on how to convince the Eskimos buy your ice.

Convincing customers to buy your products is one of the hardest things you can do. There are a number of things you need to put into play to see you succeed in your journey of convincing customers to buy your stuff.

❖ The Art Of Selling Ice To The Eskimos

❖ Laws You Need To Obey To Sell Ice Effectively To The Eskimos

Factors to Consider

➤ It is good to eliminate distractions. You will be required to be in full control of potential clients by attracting their attention. You can only achieve this is you focus on them alone and know what you want to achieve at the end of the day. It is also good to focus on an unexplored area. This is where the Eskimos have not heard of the importance of ice. These are the kind of people that you can successfully convince and sell them ice.

➤ It is good to be enthusiastic. It will be of great importance if you will be enthusiastic about the importance of your ice to the Eskimos. This is one great way of getting many customers.

➤ It is of great significance to put more concentration on how to sell. Make your decisions with emotions but then sell the ice with logic. It is good to have good preparations logically but sell with emotions. This is what will see you being aggressive to look for clients. It is good to convince the Eskimos that they will feel great if you sell them the ice. Tell them of its importance.

➤ Being direct is one thing that will see you getting more Eskimo customers to buy your products. Stop beating around the bush. Just hammer your sales ideas on the head direct. This is a good way that will see your clients say yes to your products.

How To Get The Eskimos Buy Your Ice Again And Again

As an entrepreneur who has ventured into the business of selling ice to the Eskimos, you will be demoralized if you receive a cold reception. This means the Eskimos will say no to your ice. Let the no not be the end of hope of succeeding in your business. There are a number of ways you can change this no to a yes.

It is good to be humorous. When you face the Eskimos to sell them ice, try to be humorous so that you create a rapport. Some experts in the sales industry recommend that you use phrases like, 'Thanks for saying no. I am used to three no's before I hear a yes. Do you know anybody else who can say no?' You can also use a phrase like, 'Is that your final answer?' These are phrases that will help you attract the attention of the Eskimos even if they had said no. They will link you with the Eskimos so that you get the platform of selling your ice to them.

When your Eskimos clients say no, it is good to inquire again and again until you get the main reason why they said no. Get to know the main reason why the customer said so. This is a weakness you need to take as an advantage to your side so that you work on. This will see you convince them to say yes.

It will be good to find out whom your customers buy their ice from. This will be a good way of knowing the criterion the other sellers use to convince them buy ice. Go and work on this criterion and even improve it so that next time you approach them you will automatically win them. If next times they don't buy your ice then know maybe you overworked over the same.

To ensure your customers come to buy from you again and again, make them hungry for your ice. This can be achieved if you sell them high quality ice. They will also long to buy from you if you treat them with courtesy. This can be done by:

a. Loving your customers. The first impression you show when you approach them will tell them if you love and care for their needs. Many customers will like to do business with people who care about their needs. These are the people who will know what their exact problem is and deliver the right solution.

b. Addressing your customers by name will be a good way of motivating them to do business with you. This is one of the magical tools that many people in the business industry have used to attract more customers. This is a show that you are interested in knowing them. This will make them feel free to buy your ice.

c. If you want to keep customers, it will be of great importance to be fast in your actions. You need to offer them instant responses to their problems. This is what will build trust in them about what you are selling. Try to explain to them how your ice will save them from the bondage of problems they are in.

d. It is good to adhere and fulfill your promises to the Eskimos. There is nothing which will turn off customers like when you don't keep your promises. If you promise to offer a solution to a given problem by a certain time, try to do that. If you can't, try to give a tangible reason as to why you can't. This will be a great way of enabling your customers to come again and again.

Chapter 5

Secrets on How to Sell Ice to the Eskimos

"That person is so good at sales; they could sell ice to Eskimos." This is a common saying that is used to describe someone who is good at sales.

A good sale person is one who can sell anything to anybody at any time. This means you should be able to convince people buy what you want. You can achieve this by having confidence of approaching them.

❖ Steps Of Selling Ice To The Eskimos

❖ Good Salesmen Insights On Marketing Products

Secrets

Picture of confidence courtesy of inspirationblogpost.com

Confidence is one thing that will make you gain the courage and be fluent is explaining your ideas to people. When you have confidence in what you engage in, you will be in a better position to convince your customers buy your stuff.

The main question that will guide you through the whole process of selling ice t the Eskimos is: Why am I interested in selling ice to Eskimos? If you get the answer to this question then you will be at a good position to sell your products to your destined customers.

Steps Of Selling Ice To The Eskimos Step 1:

Make sure you expose the problem. This is the first thing you need to do. Show the people you want to sell your products to that they have a certain problem that they need to work and eliminate.

Explain how your products will be very crucial to help them solve the problem. By doing this, your customers will be interested to know how their problem is going to be solved.

Let you clients know that there is a full grown problem that needs to be addressed. By exposing the problem, you will be attracting clients as many people will be sorting out the solution to this problem.

Step 2:

Demonstrate the ability to offer a solution. After exposing the problem, the next thing to do is to offer a solution to your customers.

By offering solution, it means you explain to the customers how your products will help them to cater for the problem they are facing. Don't give then full information on your product but rather be in a state that shows you are sympathizing with them.

It is good to show that you are in a state of offering a solution to their problems. It is good to explain how important your solution will be to your customers. This is one way of seeing them buy your products so that they can have your problem solved. It is good to climb down to their level so that you share with them the pain.

Step 3:

Show your customers the benefits of your products. Now that you have shown them the problem and explained the need to find a solution, your next objective is to show them of what benefit will be your products to them.

When you have a problem, it is upon you to try and solve it. Solving it means you get the most appropriate way that will completely eradicate this problem. Don't show your customers what you do or offer but also show them the benefits of what you offer. Don't show them your products but rather explain to them what they will gain if they put into use your products.

Step 4:

Justify and act. Once you have provided all the information to your customers, it is time to show them the real sale. To make them buy, you will have to use your skills to convince them that your products are the best. It is good to act on the drawbacks that may come your way. You can achieve this by justifying your actions. Giving your clients a reason to buy is a good way to have more sales. Show them the need to have your products solve their problems.

Good Salesmen Insights On Marketing Products

The hardest business you can venture into is the one for selling ice to an Eskimo. A good sales man is the one who has the right skills that will see them sell any product to any people.

If you are an Eskimo, a good sales person is the one who will show you the ice, tell you every detail of it, and let you touch it, feel it, smell it and then show you the benefits of it to your life. Even if you stay in the place where you see ice each day, after the explanation you will see this ice as being different.

You will begin to see the other part of ice you have never experienced before. By the time the explanation will be done, you will be ready to buy this block of ice.

It is good to know as a sales person that some things are sold only if they are explained and implied. You can't sell something the customer is not aware of. You need to present your products so that the customers can have a look at them before subscribing to your explanations.

A good sales person should allow the customer to interact with the product so that they get to know how it works.

Some of the Eskimo sales and marketing techniques that have been used and worked magic include:

1. **Use of images for explanation**

Depending on the products you are selling, it is good to use images to further explain how the products will be of benefit to the customers. The use of images can enhance the customers' decision to buy a product you are selling. Images will tend to communicate more than you talking.

They tend to remain in the memory of customers for a long period of time. If you have a more outrageous image, you will be at a good chance of attracting many customers. Let the images used be humorous and appealing.

If you are for example selling lawn mowers, it is good to use the image of a lawn mower to explain how it works. This will be a good way of getting your customers buy it.

It is good to use images to show how your product is used so that it gives the customers the best services. Picture courtesy of imageenvision.com

2. Use symbolism.

Use of imagery and symbolism is one thing that will see you sell your products well. Sell products referring to people who use it. If for example you are selling ice use symbolism of people eating the same. Get your clients to know that ice is good.

3. It is good to convey your mood.

It will be of great importance to convey your mood through what you say. Make sure you appreciate your customers. This is a good way of setting them into the mood of doing business with you. This is one strategy you should stick to in order to attract more and more clients to buy your products.

The mood you have is the one that will determine the number of clients to buy your products. Even if you have been annoyed by different people, don't show your customers that you are. Try to smile to them and treat them with courtesy.

4. **It is good to blend the benefits into the product you are selling**

It is good to explain to your customers the benefits they will be entitled to once they purchase the products you have. You will sell your products effectively with ease if you explain the benefits vividly to the target clients.

It is good to take your time to give fully explanation as to why your clients should buy your products. Many business experts advise that you should be creative in the way you convince people to buy your stuff. This is one thing that will see your business flourish. You will be able to earn more profits if you have the right strategy.

Wrapping Up

If the best salesmen on earth are able to see the needs of needing ice among the Eskimos market, it simply means it is mindset and selling techniques that matters.

Many times we tend to assume that people do not need the things we sell but if we can make them see the values of the products or services we are selling, we are already winning the game.

With these techniques revealed in this eBook, you will be no ordinary salesman but one that who is able to sell ice to the Eskimos.

Have fun selling!

9 785204 900035

Printed by Libri Plureos GmbH in Hamburg,
Germany